billy
casper's
tears

**billy
casper's
tears**

paul summers

**STACK
BOOKS**

```

Smokestack Books
1 Lake Terrace, Grewelthorpe, Ripon HG4 3BU
e-mail: info@smokestack-books.co.uk
www.smokestack-books.co.uk

Copyright 2022, Paul Summers
ISBN 9781838465391

Cover image:
detail from *DIORAMA SS.8.67* by
Ian Stephenson, 1967

Smokestack Books
is represented by
Inpress Ltd
```

for ash & the lads

Contents

missa saecularia   11
the great refusal   12
the sleeper wakes   13
grieving in outer space   17
quake   18
the gut   19
coble   20
undertow   21
billy casper's tears   22
wreck   24
cacophony   26
st lucy's day 2016   27
fiddlers' green   28
snag   29
jihad   30
the phoney war   31
пизды   32
a storm coming   33
the spital dene fox   34
ten breaths on mussel scarp   36
rush   37
crown   38
soon   39
feud   40
your catholic smile   41
black friday   42
the age of mediocrity   44
re-union/night at the museum   45
nativity 2016   47
the riggindale eagle   48
what the shepherd told bill   49
lots of things which rhyme that i would not take with me
in the event of a planetary evacuation   50
requiem   52
autumn song   53

kiki	54
cargo	55
blanc	56
a week away from being ten	57
the emperor of sleet	58
mothers' day 2017	59
no change given	60
alchemy	61
the crows dream too	62
the hive of liberty	63
trace	64
the song of oothoon / woman in chains	66
post-partem	67
stones	68
the last post	69
until victory always	70
wunderkammer	71
#resist	72
a.s.d.	74
song for joe skipsey	75
bun stop	77
eid al fitr, 2016	79
ligne rouge	80
apollo	81
confluence	82
tynemouth saturnalia	83
on the provenance of a feather found in the gutter	84
prow	85
tríptico órgiva	86
lament	89
Bretagne	90
palmyra, ne30	91
returning	92
shiva	93
the dream of the magi	94
dark	95
naglfar	97
the dreamers' ark	98

bequest   101
the longest day   102
swell   104
lovesong   105

acknowledgements   107

missa saecularia

there is grace
in the swell
of curving light,
the bulging liminal's
cornflower blush,
in nettle & dock,
in crow-song burr,
the casual whitethroat's
perfect poise.

the great refusal

each brittle shaft
of autumn light
draughts distance
darker, ill-defined,
renders this grief
both arbitrary & vane.
the salt looks back,
retracing the wake
of the biggest adventure.
beyond the anarchy
of restless waves,
the shrinking smirk
of cold, black rock;
the basalt fists of home,
its petrified heart,
a mother's weak magic,
a tight-lipped arc,
the great refusal.

the sleeper wakes

it is almost
inaudible

drown out
by the drone

of our shopping
channel juicers

the bleat of our trauma
our narcissist blurt

the quiet slaughter
of the fattened poor

*

welcome
to my kingdom

to the fag-end
of its progress

a slow-mo flash-fire
of bubbling tar

consuming the fibres
of jaundiced filters

this autumn air
our breath incendiary

we live off fear
& borrowed hate

*

& nothing
will grow

in the shadow
of our romance

*

way off-camera
beyond the reach

of news cycles
& investigative minds

the death toll is rising
the body count grows

bruised hearts
& airless lungs

clogged arteries
& petrified tongues

passion corroded
empathy eroded

asphyxiated dreams
statistics & lies

& god is dead
the faithful fucked

their currency
devalued or defunct

our father. oh father
grant us each day

our daily pills
our snidey tabs

our red-tops
& the strongest drink

our multipack crisps
our poundshop ket

our smack & crack
our poppers & skunk

deliver us our bargain hunt
& the great british bake-off

imprison us with labels
cage us in our minds

*

we live off fear
& borrowed hate

i will smear my cell
with dogma & lard

unleash a plague
of thankless hope

*

it is almost
inaudible

through the drone
of this chatter

the movement of traffic
the transit of hours

the rumble of hunger
the hiss of the rain

the dirge of defeat's
monotonous refrain

dürer's horsemen
braying at the door

the quiet slaughter
of the fattened poor

grieving in outer space

once, still raw,
incapable of framing
the finality of death,
i told them you'd inhabit
the brightest of the stars.
today, i am frail
with the newest grief,
they pay me back
with a lie of their own,
dragging me gently
towards their world.
we build a spaceship
from half a dozen cushions.
a squeeze but functional;
a frantic communion
of limb & breath & soon
we are orbiting an unnamed
moon whose surface glows
titanium white, we wave
on each pass, our memories
resisting the freedom
to be weightless.

quake

'the old world is dying, and the new world struggles to be born:
now is the time of monsters.'

antonio gramsci

& the way will be perilous;
black ice & shark-eyed smiles,
several heaps of hogmanay vomit,
a vacant pizza-box draped with hoar,
its palimpsest of feast & greed,
bleak litany of the new & old,
dog-shit & fag-ends & crumbling roads,
the hours' lash, the pains of labour,
the endless cycle of peddled fact.
& then the sanctuary of frozen sand;
its confluence of salt & wind-whipped crows,
the hymn of a sea cathedral hollow.
kick off your shoes my love & walk;
due east, towards the burgeoning sun.
plough on through the grave mounds
of haddock-frames & listless kelp,
tread slowly on the pebble field,
avoid the triggers of its toad-back traps;
then walk & wade & catch your breath,
beyond the bar where codling lurk,
let swell becalm your troubled blood,
squeeze shut your jaded eyes & dream;
the rapture of tectonic plates entwined
in acts of violence & of love, the red raw
ooze of magma's birthing, each push,
each jolt, each breathless force exerted
sees citadels emergent from these waves,
a glimpse of doggerland's trembling plains,
its strongholds of hope re-rendered
now un-drowned, their beacons still charged,
their gates agape, their monsters slain;
each edifice an altar awaiting our faith.

the gut

north shields fish quay, easter 2020

landlocked,
a slump
of idle nets
await a fix,
form calvary
between
the lines.
a cormorant
set into a cross
imagines a sun
to warm its wings.
the creels,
stood down,
remembering function,
remembering storm.

coble

spanish battery, tynemouth

reluctantly,
a shivering crow
utters the semblance
of a blunt hello.
framed by grey,
the crabbers pray
the next pot full
& in the lull
between the haul,
the bait & set,
a moment gifted
to sweet regret.
the wind has shifted,
the swell grown loud,
her slapped percussion
on the hull & in the lull
of wane & surge,
their eyes are bowed
in quiet mourning,
entranced by the dirge
of the fog horn's warning,
their losses replete:
each narrow defeat,
some love forsaken,
the road not taken,
their promise spurned,
the bridges burned,
a crust unearned.
the tide has turned.

undertow

a fractious coven
of pristine gulls

subsisting on mizzle
& the echo of their cackle.

we build frail cairns
to house our ghosts,

each flimsy stack
a shrine to transience.

north of rapture.
north of grief.

concealed inside
each measured tide,

the skulking
undertow of home.

billy casper's tears

i.m. darrin john rudd

immaculate,
above the prow,
a kestrel strains
against the gale;

grace dispensed
to break its fast,
it takes a dunnock
on the wing.

the rocks lament
their slow decay
each tide unpicks
their knotted lore,

unmakes this version
of themselves,
all frail nostalgia
undermined.

sleek as grief
another bleak
cadaver sky
lets loose its spells;

the fleeting scrawl
of hungry terns
deface the grey
with distant names,

each curving volley
of icy rain
dissolves to ghosts
within its murk,

involuntary,
unending,
like billy casper's
quiet tears.

wreck

the black middens, tynemouth

a rat looks on
at a sinking ship;
perplexed by the volume
of their growing agitation.
snow is silent,
or so they say.
that night, it screamed,
beseeching mothers
& some god's mercy.
that night, it wretched
in brackish cold,
it gargled froth
from drowning lungs.
a girl breaks surface;
accepts the basalt's
loveless kisses.
a girl breaks surface,
close to the split
of a fractured hull,
grabs greedily
at plangent air.
she catches a snowflake
in the whiteness of her fist.
she beckons to the rat.
he turns his back;
the deadweight
of her petticoat
dragging her back under.
snow is silent,
or so they say.
that night, it wailed
in thankless grief,
howled out

in wanton disbelief
that death could claim
these thirty-four
just half a furlong
from the shore.

cacophony

june 2016

beyond the bleat
of our descent

the slur of hatreds
a tumult of fears

the crackle of gunfire
& cold white noise

the hum of our frailty
each lisping distraction

the hiss of mute daylight
invading our borders

i crave the welcome
of a colony of moss

the gentle union
of our troubled skin

st lucy's day 2016

daybreak is washed
with syrian blood

a thicket of cloud
will belch its grief

this air a salve
of salt & weed

of wailing gulls
& narrow breath

light has trawled
a skein of swans

the flip-book flicker
of dissonant wings

the wind against them
their progress scant

fiddlers' green

invisible,
the gulls' hysterics.

the ferry departs.
a baritone horn

left lingering
in curdled fog.

i think of losses,
the concept of distance.

snag

there is darkness
in the wheeze
of the season's haste.
the clouds, a bruise,
the early blooms
have gone to seed,
the anchor snagged
in the comfort of denial;
i comb a thistle's tatted hair.

jihad

how quickly
we resort to hate

recklessly acceptant
of its every invitation

all fear predated
tenderness un-feted

the puzzle of our rage
translated into carnage

beneath the orbit
of a tolling bell

these snow-drops
lead a merry dance

the joy of their distraction
set fragile & short-lived

the phoney war

england, july 2016

drip

drip

drip

un-danceable
this rhythm

each poisoned kiss
a gloss for the gutter

this metronome
of cycled news

funereal & scant
no beauty in it

tarkovsky meets goebbels
dogma meets spite

the milk is spilled
the cat un-bagged

take me to the mountain
with all of its magic

пизды

*'it is easier to forgive an enemy
than to forgive a friend.'*
                              william blake

here, in the reek of treachery's lair,
squat lancelot & brutus & tony blair;
their contract with their demons made,
their standards ripped, their cause
betrayed. their dark conceits fresh hell
will claim, their faces masked by cauls
of shame. we, who piss against the wind
have spent the currency of an age to tame
the behemoth of our adolescent rage;
then just as faith reclaims its prey:
the desperate, the guilty, the death-bed
believer; our loathing finds renaissance
with the fervency of fever.

a storm coming

stillborn, this light
makes reason heresy,
casts kindness lame.

this blue lipped sky
impeaching hope
to brutal inquisition;

resilience snagged
on the spelks
of crow-song,

the waves a knot
of curtailed passage,
the cobles beached.

the spital dene fox

the sky is the belly
of a spawning trout

each cloud-dance driven
by instinct & intent

above this sweep
of shivering sea

a squall has dragged
a splaying brush

obtuse & acute
a thatch of light

a season blooming
in its delicate touch

a ripening bruise
of icy rain

each surge short-lived
each break profane

through cataracts
of frozen breath

we read the melody
of her trace

a filigree libretto
transcribed in hoar

a confluence
of grace & awe

betrays a fox-trot's
slick dynamics

her transit bulging
in nervous arcs

a moment won
to taste the air

the pockmarks
of a distant stare

her hunger replete
a staged retreat

a rusted ghost
dissolved by dawn

ten breaths on mussel scarp

for mark johnston

exhale the breath of war
the heft of prescience

the sanderlings lead
their merry dance

venerate the sheen of silt
make idols of the lost & found

a home bargains trolley
uninjured by its fall

a five ounce sinker
a filleter's glove

the saturated bulb
of a dark-wood pipe

a lifeless starfish
an action man head

his drowning eyes
kissed shut by kelp

a razor shell
a bovine tooth

ten green bottles
none with a message

rush

9 furlongs out,
beyond the bar,
our grief inhabits
the arc of distance.

we look beyond
the curve of air,
find solace in
the breath of clouds.

this promontory
a fertile flush
of carragheen
& bladderwrack;

of ink-blue mussel,
& humbug snail,
of wader, of gull
& hungry rat.

they greet the tide
with welcome kisses,
draw prospect from its
boisterous in-rush.

crown

cormorants haunt
this cataract haze,

i set my breath
in time with waves.

the gulls engaged
in ceremonials

crown me king
of all i survey:

protector of the winkle,
custodian of kelp,

friend of the rat
& nervous crab;

each oath anointed
by brackish tide.

soon

there is solace in moss
slow grace imparted
in the fern's unfurling

the stoat throws off
his winter coat
a season melts

the birds unmuted
each bud expectant
a carillon of lapis bells

feud

beyond the hump
of violet distance,
the threat of rain
waits crouching
on its honkers.
frail with rage
a gaunt quartet
of hungry crows
have turned on
themselves;
& sensing blood,
or threat of it,
another dozen
swells the mob.
hate in the beads
of jaundiced eyes.
their raucous curses
dissolved by tide.
today, at least,
it comes to nothing.

your catholic smile

i.m. r m mckay

it is dusk
on the scarp

redshanks bleat
their staid laments

the light infirm
re-polishes the silt

a dead-slow tides'
tubercular wheeze

mimics the gossip
of distant trees

i have walked for a year
this same cold mile

trawling the half-light
for your catholic smile

black friday

grey-scale thursday
dies un-fêted

opiate numbed
our veins will sigh

gouching in the glow
of the altars of inertia

voracity replete
denial complete

there is blood
on the carpet

a pair of hipster
clones in tweed

have lost their cool
& come to blows

firstly over beard-oil
then gruffalo slippers

our fathers entrenched
amidst the toys

have wrapped themselves
with lego walls

a woman whose cheeks
are fuller than her bags

has taken a tumble
near handicrafts & festive fun

prostrate in her ecstasy
the whiff of compensation

a halo of haberdash
& miscellaneous buttons

looks like her pelvis
but i'm no doctor

outside in the garden
of earthly delights

an obese dog
looks proudly

at a pyramid
of pristine shit

both are steaming
in the coldness of the fall

the age of mediocrity

it came by stealth
though some invited
it came disguised
as friend & kin
it walked right in
& crept like plague
through all the rooms
we'd kept as sacred
each town consumed
each citadel complicit
no cell immune
the cure redacted
all grace usurped
all hope infected
the mediocre's
bleak contagion
each fertile thought
remapped as fallow
each mind re-drawn
in bland enclosures
their promise stacked
in putrid piles
bequeath the meek
this palsied earth

re-union/night at the museum

the wallaw, blyth

'*spoons*' is stowed;
its crowded bar
a wedge of thirst,
an eager slick
of growing agitation,
a confluence of
unhealed wounds,
a tumour of attrition,
a smudged tattoo
whose weeping edges
relish in contagion.
we worship at the altar
of the cut-price crowd,
blunt sepulchre
of misplaced faith,
a reliquary of losses
& every empty victory,
of stagnant empire's
tattered standards,
of struggle & toil,
of all our dead parents
& awkward divorces,
of capped shafts
& yards left idle,
of empty shops
& factories grown quiet
of rotting staithes,
of thrift & forgetting,
of youth & truth,
of every scant memorial.
communion
in the trauma
of a century's neglect.

we meet to remember.
the absurd theatre
of our former selves,
a wake for our imagined pasts.
we drink it all in,
raise toasts to the absent
& to all our frail futures,
whose faces have grown grey
through scarcity of care.
here, where empties
form a barricade
across the bar;
bleak jäger-bombs
explode like hope
above our heads,
each sickly shot
a warning from history.
we cultivate our spite,
our rhetoric primed,
cementing our dogmas
in monoliths of settled dust.
once, within
these flickering walls
we learned our fear
of sharks & war,
our love of love,
the warmth of kisses,
curled like cats
in dark back rows
beneath an arrowhead
of magic light.

nativity 2016

the manger
transformed:

a callous nest
of smouldering spelks

& swaddling cloth,
of roasted bone

& rendered flesh.
the magi weep,

depleted by
their journey.

*we bring a balm
of dust & blood,*

*a flask of brine,
this infant to anoint.*

the riggindale eagle

drip weak sun
on lifeless wings;

drape him a shroud
from mizzle & scree.

each plume,
un-preened,

submissive to the hiss
of this paschal squall.

the last great eagle
of cumberland dead.

limp of nape
& cloudy of eye,

his talons splayed,
his curse undone.

freed of the yoke
of hollow breath,

this decade of hours
grown dank & elastic,

each thankless sky-dance
drawn blank & unrequited.

what the shepherd told bill

the owl purveys
its wit to who?
the pastor to
an empty pew?
a sermon to comfort
the chosen few?

the word falls mute
beyond the choir;
the flock dispersed
amidst the mire,
hock-deep they trudge
let fate transpire.

faithful to the folly
of antecedent trace.
let bards bear
witness to this place,
chronicle the anguish
in each ovine face.

re-learn the language
of the herd, re-tell its tales.
lead them home by heart
& head, not by their tails.
when trusted by our charges
the good shepherd prevails.

lots of things which rhyme that i would not take with me in the event of a planetary evacuation

capitalism / cataclysm /narcissism / catechism / the march of
neo-liberalism / the anuretic embolism /the new managerial /
anything imperial / confederate flags /louis vuitton bags /
received pronunciation / blatant acts of ingratiation /
starvation / stagnation / exploitation / alienation /
deforestation / non-consensual penetration / vacuous wankers
/ merchant bankers /homeopaths / psychopaths / intolerance /
ignorance / sycophants / fire ants / leopard print nylon
underpants / jewellery made from elephants / sebaceous cysts
/ misogynists / cultural colonialists / predatory recidivists /
ukes / nukes / tv cooks / martin amis books /eating disorders /
constructed borders / child abuse / the hangman's noose / the
original soundtrack of footloose / poetry's recourse to the
needlessly obtuse / domestic violence / that awkward silence
/posh physicians / teenage magicians /endless conversations
about yoga positions / inane blogs / yappy dogs / referring to
the french as frogs / ads for hot ukrainian brides / unrelenting
genocides / murdering bees with pesticides / klu klux klans /
obsessions with le creuset pans / royal babies / rabies / quorn
/porn / the mediocre / online poker / chicken pox / botox /
vox pops/ gm crops / death / bad breath / crystal meth / every
tory shibboleth / orange pith /the beauty myth / fracking /
hacking / smacking / academies with corporate backing /
dementia / involuntary indenture / racial tension /
condescension / slaves to convention/ middle class pretension
/ hipster poseurs / brown nosers / various cancers / politicians'
bland non-answers / sweat shops /racist cops / bullington club
fops/ red tops /chieftain tanks / food-banks / alt right cranks /
voluminous yanks / endless war / geordie shore / assassin
drones / mobile phones / marble-gobbed sloans / pay day
loans / holocaust deniers / bearded messiahs / fake news / high
heeled shoes / herpes/ fleas / processed cheese/ unregulated
monopolies / extortionate tuition fees / the inhumane

treatment of refugees / crippling debt / buy to let /
innumerable offensive smells / pharmaceutical cartels /
sleeping rough / acting tough / gratuitous swearers / rolex
wearers / judgemental starers/ the burden endured by unpaid
carers / apartheid regimes/ facebook memes / suburban semis
with fake tudor beams / boulevards of broken dreams / bilious
spite / the supremacy of white / posturing with military might
/ rupert murdoch peddling shite / the unfree state / stifled
debate / the ugliness of wanton hate / our continued
subservience to the notion of fate

requiem

i.m. aurelio borini

fox bark
& curlew hymn.

we conjure ghosts
in blushing dusk.

the tide is slack,
relishing in idle time,

an hour to fathom
the puzzle of inertia.

& limpet-pocked,
the basalt squats,

its skin as warm
as fresh laid eggs.

we sit a while
& watch the sky

each quiet breath
a wordless prayer.

autumn song

the wind is hard
& from the east

a drizzle dervish
whipped to frenzy

shrouding brambles'
swollen bellies

the swallows flee
this season of ghosts

the leaves begin
their jaundiced march

towards the days
of shrinking light

towards the nights
of frost in bloom

kiki

kiki morton
has got one arm;
the other sliced
off by a tankie's
blunt wheel,
playing chicken
on the freight-line
near malvins road.
that summer was hot;
each day elastic.
today, in the blue,
the terns chant his name,
skimming each syllable
across the glare.

cargo

grey-lipped,
another dream

grows cold,
seeks refuge

in the morgue's
bleak steel.

prospect slain,
a grief replete,

the scantest hope
reduced to meat.

blanc

today, this river
robbed of distance

its wraith cartography
consigned to our ears

sanderling & curlew
defining it edges

the fog-horn boom
the breath of tide

a solitary gull
imagining blue

a week away from being ten

between a gobful
of fish-finger

& a forkful of peas,
some rare good news.

our youngest son
in love with grace,

smitten by kindness
& fragile smiles.

he has lost all focus
in spelling & grammar,

joyously distracted
in mental math.

he can't explain it.
neither can i.

the emperor of sleet

wallsend

the billet hearth
retreats to ash,
its flicker dulled.
i dream the plains
of friesland green,
my children's breath,
my wife's warm curves,
my mother's smile;
grief's battalions unrelenting.
tomorrow we march,
the next day too,
lost in the rhythm
of our advancement;
we learn another word for cold.

mothers' day 2017

the sky defies
the rule of thirds

shields evolving from
the haar's last laugh

kingdom of winkle
& hollow whelk

of kelp's forked tongues
strewn tanned & polished

the carcass of a thorny ray
his world upended

the sea remade
resists nostalgia

& carefully tied
to a rusting rail

a jaundiced rose
in tender bondage

no change given

the news is no less shit
when wrapped in sun

the taste of loss still
sour as an unripe plum

a hemisphere can't shift
the weight of death

or else of dying
hope face down

& drowned again
in puddles of infernal

spring & me still waiting
on lenin's slow train

alone & forlorn & in
the grip of northern rain

april's thesis
still unproclaimed

jerusalem postponed
our flags left maimed

no chink of paltry light
to grace our days

all vigour subjected
to unspecified delays

alchemy

for narbi price

on freestone point
all time dissolves,
melting in the brine
of the middle wave's spittle.
each stubborn rock,
reluctant but complicit,
contemplates its passage
to dune or bar.
distance is a line
of tailors' chalk,
our futures poised
in its arc's slick magik.
the heft of cloud
compressing light,
conjuring violet
from whispered white.

the crows dream too

the crows dream too
of hunger & joy

of fear & stars
of truths corroded

fantasia's seduction
nostalgia's corruption

each narrative feathered
by the rigor of a gale

the hive of liberty

for old tom spence

Gŏd gav thĭ Ir'th too u
And nŏt unto a Fu
Bŭt aul Mănkind

& still we build
drone & dreamer

beyond each epoch's
bleak indenture

making & amending
each pristine cell

to house the progeny
of our rights

a scaffold thatch
of vehement words

the lathe & daub
of hope & want

each glossed with the blood
of a ranter's raw throat

trace

for nev clay

today, the sea,
clad head to toe

in winter's rage
rakes up the past;

roaring out
her bleak unwelcome.

baits the scavengers
with her loot:

the maudlin
& the po-face crow;

unearths the trace
of loss & gain,

of lust, of death,
of moments unfinished,

of labours' pain,
& the searingly mundane.

the tooth of an ox
who had fawned over sunsets,

the sole of a shoe
that had walked on gold,

a broken mast,
it's core still straining

with the tempest's
blunt memory,

a pipe still warm
from a docker's cracked lips,

a vulcanite stopper
infused with their thirst,

the polished bones
of man & beast,

each spur & burr
filed off by time.

today, the sea,
clad head to toe

in winter's rage
rakes up the past;

the redshanks bleat
their false alarms,

my pockets bulge
with weighty votives.

the surfers wait,
still poised to catch

that perfect wave
which never comes.

the song of oothoon/woman in chains

'The daughters of Albion hear her woes, and echo back her sighs'
William Blake

hail the virgin of the waves
sacred in her violation,

staring out at hope's fresh grave,
still fettered by a man's volition.

bruised & torn, she tends her grief,
enveloped by the jaded surf,

anoints the construct of her shame
with menstrual blood & sorrow's brine.

a crown of sins, a crown of thorns,
all innocence usurped by time,

the wreckage of her freedom strewn
between the loud & the tormented.

in bondage to their malediction,
chattel of their rank abuses.

post-partem

coalburn cottage, eglingham. 1811

piteous, the baby cries
hollow lips that crave the teat

& mother's mouth
reverts to tongues

she counts the diamonds
on an adder's back

a fever to warm
the chill of home

transform this rough-shod crib
into a cist of chalky bones

nanna mary drops her head
all her wisdom & her herbs

rendered useless by these hours
the tallow sags & now they pray

stones

the rievers & the balladeers
assemble now to build a cairn

a gathering in gloaming light
to lay to rest a stillborn bairn

the last post

an ode to facebook

white noise in the echo room.
language in spate yet wisdom
thirsts. our reason strangled
by tangled fact. the howl of
the emptied & the great unheard.
the grieving & the wronged.
the hollow men & clowns.
our rage drum-hollow. our
laughter cast mute. a slurry
of trauma & smiling kittens.
the pouting wounds of love
& loathing. the peony blooms
& blood red moons. nostalgia
& narcissus. gun-crime & gaza
& walnut tortellini. flags & tits
& hotel pools. the lost & found.
the righteous bleat of the boho
sages. sweet opiate communion.
emoji heart. emoji heart. our smiles
subservient to status & shares.

until victory always

between black friday
& cyber monday

between the poles
of hope & defeat

a hair's breadth
a last breath

the forked tongue
of the sabbath

the veiled threat
of advent

of fingers burnt
in chanukah flames

we wear our dogma
like a shroud

your ashes scattered
in the bay of pigs

still we wait
& still we sing

like stubborn leaves
resisting the fall

wunderkammer

nettle flower
& deer trace

petrichor
& curlew

moon-shadow
& virgin snow

the sacred marriage
of light & water

the breath of clouds
& pin-prick mizzle

puffin beak
& fern unfurling

a dew-soaked gansie
knitted from cobwebs

#resist

he's off the tabs
& off the drink.

two days into
a miracle diet

that saved some wee lad
in rural scandinavia.

he'd seen it in *hello*,
on monday, at the barbers.

the nag has bolted,
all truth be told.

the doc says he's fucked
or words to that effect.

his emphysema's
not for turning.

his liver transformed
to shippam's paste.

a case of when not if.
a time to start giving

a bit of thought to which
neil young song he wants

playing at the crem
& who'll do the buffet,

a time to make peace
with his brother, the copper.

& slumped in the bucket
of his da's old armchair,

his attention is divided
between micro & macro:

gramsci's prison notebooks
& a mobility scooter catalogue.

he contemplates the future,
with half an eye on bargain hunt;

wrestling with hegemony
& the puzzle of complicity.

a.s.d.

beneath a super-moon
obscured by cloud

our dance is quick,
each gleeful step

anoxic & misplaced,
our balance skewed,

our mouths agape
in idiot grins.

between the migration trends
of late cretaceous herbivores

& the approximate diameter
of the sea of tranquillity,

the monarch of fact,
an equation for love.

song for joe skipsey

speared by a volley
of icy rain

the pitman bard
of percy main

seeks solace
in his tired brain

wrestles the cadence
of verse & refrain

finds grief in the heave
of jet-black seams

to poison the heart
of a poet's dreams

grief in the threnody
of creaking props

in the residue of silence
when breathing stops

in the fatal trace
of a peelers' bullet

lodged like injustice
in his father's gullet

in cribs left vacant
by fever's rage

within the lines
of creeping age

within the spite
that is wed to class

within the fault-lines
of mirrored glass

within the reek
of the tyne's foul breath

within the struggle
of life & death

bun stop

hail the starlings
of amen corner,
their anarchy
tamed by the pulse
of murmuration.

hail the melody
of stone & brick,
of bulging glass,
these jaded domes
& gilded spires.

hail the rhythms
of footfall & heart,
the blood & sweat
of struggles spent
& yet to pass.

hail the tension
in this puddle's skin,
the fragile dialectic
of gravity & mass,
its face bow-taut,
each stance conflicted.

hail to the hoar
on the cobble's pout,
these gutters choked
with poet's whimsy,
hubris & votives,
rhetoric floundering
in the lort burn's swill.
hail sycophant & sage,
the muddle of denial,
cold land of lad

& bloated laird,
of thrones usurped
or quietly vacant.

hail these bridges
& the arc of their stature.
hail the municipal
& the muted keep.

hail snowdrop & bluebell
& the toll of our losses.
republic of goose-bump
& high street dandy,
fiefdom of magpie
& impotent ghosts;
each spurt of growth
constricted by romance.

hail this dance
of scant advancement,
the cadence of decay
in the tyne's chill madrigal.
confluence of meme & gene;
each artery clogged.

hail the kittiwakes
of spillers' mill,
proclaiming their prayer
to fractured dawn,
a clutch of notes
to do their bidding.

eid al fitr, 2016

the moon has crowned,
revealed its pristine fontanel

& gaunt with grief, a wailing man
repeats his children's empty names;

their corpses & their prospects limp,
a pail of tears to swill away the blood & flame.

a breath away, we savour a second
in the slurry of our progress;

slow grace evolved in gloom,
a fragile moment of pristine warmth,

the tender union of skin & air,
the radiant amber of a slug's fallen hem,

the burn in spate, the anarchy of cloud,
the sky in free-fall, our gods dishonoured.

ligne rouge

for john berger

draw me a line
blunt in this sand

all form dictated
by the weight of days

fluid & free-wristed
the bulge of our losses

a love underscored
an error struck-through

the limb of each draught
made sure & unflinching

the awkward curve
of truth's gaunt lips

the flush of the liminal
in cadmium red

apollo

peterlee, co. durham

i knew two lads
from sunny blunts

this future painted
them as hopeless cunts

devoid of prospect, all at sea
the poor lost boys of peterlee

apprenticed in this concrete
familiar with each brutal node

the borstal spots upon their hands
became an undecipherable code

a narrative of battle scars
of bleak red lines & burnt out cars

they cooked up oblivion
in pasmore's pavilion

confluence

a furlong beyond
the pincer grip
of pier & pier,
the bulges of
a subtle line
for whom la peste
will hold no fear.
a confluence
to underscore
the construct
of our distance;
a marriage forced
upon itself:
of rusted iron
& tired steel,
of tenderness
& seething rage,
of red & black,
of tyne & tide.
a moveable feast,
oblivious to audience,
their fingers knotted,
in pristine union.

tynemouth saturnalia

beyond the middens'
proudest peak,
where limpets sculpt
their cups & rings,
just fish-bone & whelk
& wave-thrown clay,
the raw divinity
of crow & gull.
beyond the scarp,
the reach of men
diminished
to a flimsy dream,
the stab of grief
to nettle sting.
here a saint might
make his god
& demons their legion;
each strike of tide
re-forging faiths.

on the provenance of a feather found in the gutter

wrestling with his pillow
icarus dreams of falling

an angel plummeting
through thinnest air

not fear but rapture
impervious to impact

neither ego nor grace
know much of weight

the rooks dispose
of his broken corpse

& history will restart
its essence conserved

provoked into rhythm
like a faltering heart

prow

spanish battery, tynemouth

only the grace
of flickering tide

the air alight
with foist & fox

all time is here
each stolen hour

left mute & captive
within these rocks

tríptico órgiva

i

dawn has your eyes.
the sun, an altar
& roses bow.
the miner & his lover
kiss in their cave:
mouth on mouth,
tongue on tongue,
lips on skin,
lips on fingers.
love is the spring
which quenches their thirst.
love is the cook
who feeds their bellies.
they live on the mountain.
they live on the margins.
some days they cry.
grief is a bird
that will not leave the nest.
pain is the boar
who blocks their path.
joy is the hare
he cannot snare.
they live on the mountain.
they kiss in their cave.

ii

day kicks off his shoes,
throws down his clothes,
stands at a window
& thinks for a moment.
only the cicada's
electric hiss,
only the water's
stuttering dance;
a chorus of dogs erupting
like a smoker's cough.
the mountain twitches
in its sleep.
the lovers embrace.
the stars blink.

iii

the moon & the flower
are dancing in the garden;

oblivious to audience,
contented in their silence.

the flush of their skins
have coalesced,

they sway to the rhythm
of empty time.

tonight, the mountain
is soaked with blood,

draped in the wheeze
of breathless trees.

the moon & the flower
are blind to its suffering;

indifferent to pain.
they are dancing in the garden;

rubbing salt in the wounds
of our broken little hearts.

lament

alfacar, 18 august 1936

'*i want to sleep the sleep of apples*'
frederico garcia lorca

hear it tumble
down to viznar:

the echo of
the rifles' volley,

the echo of
a monster's cackle,

seeping through
the olive groves.

a spring of blood,
a weave of limbs,

the anarchy
of death's contortion,

the thirsty dirt
gagging their protest.

the swallows weep,
the saints impotent,

the grieving moon,
prostrate at his feet.

Bretagne

red stars still hang
high over douarnenez

silenced by time
& made redundant

the cursed poets
gather near the quay

conversing through drink
& the blueness of smoke

meticulous as sparrows
they cultivate their lines

each tender gesture
each exquisite pain

snagged in the mesh
of the old blue nets

palmyra, ne30

today, the sea
is dirtied jade,
a bruise of cloud
above the pier.
someone
has smashed
my latest cairn
to smithereens.
the air still heavy
with need & rage,
the trace of suffering;
each flattened stone
reduced to pigment.
i grieve a while,
then build another
in its footprint,
fond of gestures
of stubborn hope.
the crows will pose
their awkward questions,
i think on sea-snails:
their knotted passage,
how all our learning
becomes unraveled.
today, the sea
is dirtied jade,
a bruise of cloud
above the pier.

returning

the codling are back,
ghosting through
the amber kelp;
savouring the cold
on the arc
of their flanks.
the sky has the hue
of a dead man's lips,
a rib of dense cloud
advancing from the west.
a brace of curlews
forage on the skeer,
busy with subsistence,
contented to repeat
their threnody
unbounded.

shiva

the season's first hoar
lies fragile on the sand

chanukah's flames
are naked in the day

three orphans converge
their losses in confluence

each of them will pray
in their separate way

three pillars of grief
assemble on gehonom's shore

each frozen stone
a day of mourning

each frozen stone
a year, a life

the dream of the magi

the cathedral of saint lazare, autun, france

how do they sleep
knowing what they know?

how can each dream
be thus contained?

when mine run wild
each visited by awe.

how do they lie
untroubled by this hope?

their hearts at ease,
i feel it with my hand,

their eyelids a weld
of truth & faith,

forged from the down
of angels' wings.

dark

'In den finsteren Zeiten,
wird da auch gesungen werden?
Da wird auch gesungen werden.
Von den finsteren Zeiten.'

Bertolt Brecht

& on the eighth day
there was darkness
again. even darker
than the last time
but not a patch on
the next if you believe
that weird, little god-nik
fucker at the monument.
darker than that time
you gaffer taped my eyes.
darker than that night
we hammered the poitín
in davy's da's shed & you
bit off the ears of his sister's
classroom gerbil. darker
than the entire contents
of johnny cash's wardrobe.
darker than the core of an
overlooked verruca. dark
as fuck, apart from a pulse
of weak, pale light emitted
in the west from the burnt-
out convoy of overturned
police-vans currently blocking
all six lanes of the A1(M) in both
directions, & from jimmy upstairs,
who has somehow rigged an old
black & white portable to a car-
battery so he can watch *attheraces*

completely unimpeded by events
of global significance, & your
slightly eccentric, europhile
neighbour; the one with the nice
job & the buy-to-let mortgage,
engaged in an act of quiet
immolation there in the back-lane,
precariously close to our wheelie-bin.
apart from all that though, it's dark
as fuck. much darker than the last time,
not a patch on the next.

naglfar

i am the bilge rat
on the ship of nails,

trawling this swill
for sustenance & truth.

the tide lies slack;
i dig & scrat,

strike blood pacts
with the silt & stones,

whilst picking through
her fractured bones.

the curlews mourn,
my senses sail,

they voyage the void
of dead & living,

conjuring ghosts,
who speak their names.

a craft which hauled
both kings & coals

transformed into
a ship of souls.

her rudder lame,
her rotten keel

she cuts a wake
to scar my dreams.

the dreamers' ark

the haven, tynemouth

the oak is seasoned
the sawyers done

each board & beam
is shaved & steamed

rendered immaculate
in barrel curves

planed & polished
to perfect laps

the wrights slip-
glazed by noble toil

each limb in balance
each peg set tight

like lovers' vows
immoveable in situ

caulked with hope
& dogma pitched

our lines are tied
the mast is set

beyond the lash
of briny rain

the sirens call
a kelpie chorus

in refrain beseeches
us to join them

on their barricade
of angry waves

then truths & lies
file two by two

the ghosts of all
our champions too

then faith & doubt
complete the crew

the flexing muscle
of a lunatic tide

will raise us off
our silt-kissed keel

our petards primed
the mainsail draped

we'll voyage toward
some promised land

towards a haven
of our communion

this ark of gesture
& good intent

within the warp
& weft of oily sheets

the reek of sheep
the thrill of transit

its canvas chest
heaved out in pride

repels the barrage
of this storm

its swell embellished
with gilded words

non nocere
do no harm

bequest

this product counts as one of your 5-a-day

the heirloom bowl
has acquired a crack,

a hair-line supplement
to the chip on its shoulder;

a border imposed
between two blooms,

their flaccid petals
conjuring the halcyon,

a pride of place
in sabbath's dim parlour.

i have never liked maling,
its palette too garish

& all it holds, its blunt consignment,
an anxious clutch of sour grapes.

the longest day

the sun is fake news;
luring the hipsters
to hunt out espadrilles
& ice-cooled ciders.
slave to the rigours
of her lunar obligations,
the sea, grown weary,
eternally deprived of sleep;
reluctantly whips up a swell,
her choir of waves
reduced to whispers.
this maudlin light
throws down her shade,
redraws the detail
of some blunt townscape:
the cathedral of mistrust,
the morgue of hope,
the grey necropolis of dreams,
the cold panopticon
of incarcerated fact,
the bleak infirmary
of all our passion.
a billion blunt faces
roughly rendered
from a low-cost amalgam
of grief & mediocrity:
their deafened ears, wax-sealed,
their cheek-bones ignoble,
their mouths agape,
their eyes unseeing.
in scarcity of certainty,
we relish in constants:
the stairwell at wetherspoons
rife with the perfumes
of debt & burnt chips,

the till-queue at aldi
resplendent with the glow
of defeated northern smiles,
& outside the co-op,
the yokes of our apathy,
abundant as leaves.

swell

impatient, the tide
pre-empts the clock
re-drowns the skeer
with brackish cold
defies the almanac's
stubborn forecast
a full clean hour
before its time
my path is blocked.
i watch a crow
unpick the puzzle
of an awkward clam
i watch the wake
of distant transit,
its energy dissipate
on porous stones
imagine the blades
of an osprey's claws
raking the surface
of this casual swell.

lovesong

today, the sky's
an obese cadaver's
lumpen thigh,
mottled & putrid,
devoid of reflex.
out there, beyond
this brine-etched
window's bird-shit
atlas, someone
grieves & lovers kiss.
a child asks why
& none of our answers
can ever suffice.
a fragile crocus
erupts to a pout.
the rooks will polish
their jet conspiracy,
& i am weighing
the heft of our love,
wrestling its scope
into something
i can fathom.
a century of seasons
pass so quick
& still your touch
can make me reel;
can melt me like
the frailest hoar,
pluck hope like doves
from empty hats.
& i have told this
to the mountain,
to the peewits
& the gorse.
i have told it

to the flames
of a slow-dying fire,
to the bulges
of a burn in gargling
spate, but not to you
for quite some time.
a hundred brief seasons
can pass so quick.
our lives to dust
without much effort.
with the latter in mind,
i am telling you now.

acknowledgements

Firstly, thanks are due to Andy Croft & Smokestack Books for supporting & publishing my work for the last decade or so.

Thanks also to the editors of the following publications where some of these poems first appeared: *The Lake, Dreich, Ofi Press* (Mexico), *Tuck* (USA), *Sea/Film, Fat Damsel, Glove, Culture Matters, the recusant, Militant Thistles, The Pitman Poet of Percy Main, Tyne Anew, William Blake at the Bridge Hotel, Communist Party Centenary Anthology, Pawnedland, The Long White Thread of Words, Words for the Wild* and *New Boots and Pantisocracies*.

Many of these poems also appeared in the pamphlets *the boy who stole the curate's egg* (black light engine room) & *the dreamer's ark* (blueprint poetry press).

'bunstop' is taken from the filmpoem of the same name, 'the sleeper wakes' was used in the filmpoem *advent*, both were directed by Dan Douglas.

Thanks to Rob Walton for friendship, laughter & editorial advice.

Last but not least, thanks to Kate & Steve Stephenson for their continued support & friendship & for granting permission to use, a detail from 'Diorama SS.8.67' (1967) by Ian Stephenson as the cover image of this collection. For more information on Ian Stephenson & his work please visit http:www.ianstephenson.net